REVULSION FREED FROM A HEAD LOCK

(after Desire Caught By The Tail)

By

Anthony David Padgett

Published by

ADP Publishing

First Published 2019

Dedication

To

PICASSO

FOREWORD

During my artistic project "A Year With Picasso" I created over 100 paintings looking at the work and life of Pablo Picasso. The project culminated in a sculpture of the artist as a child in Malaga. Along with the sculpture are masks of Picasso as a young and old man. The paintings helped me to get an insight into Picasso. And from this I was able to see how vast and diverse his body of work was.

"Revulsion Freed From A Headlock" is my response to his main surreal play, published in 1945 "Desire Caught By The Tail". A history and analysis of the significance of his play is not the purpose of this introduction. Rather, I would like to give you an understanding of my methodology.

As my title suggests, it is an inversion of his work. My methodology in art is to look for what has not been done. And one of the tools I use for this is inversion. For instance, in my paintings I looked at Picasso and Braque's Cubism (with its straight lines and angles) and created my own Curveism.

My inversion of script in this play also involves creative choices that are not always a precise inversion. This is to make the text flow more successfully. And I also change some aspects to give them a 21st century relevance.

I hope that you will find the result interesting, and in places extraordinary.

An example of my writing that follows is:

"The impersonality of shopping through a self-service till is awful and commonplace. The lifeless, humourless coldness of the shopping, empty of love and, from start to finish, a revolting violence."

Picasso's original text (from Sir Roland Penrose's 1970 translation) is:

"Apart from the pitch or the glue of her attentions, nothing can equal her allure and her chopped flesh on the dead calm of her regal movements. Her sprightly jokes, her warmth and her chill stuffed with hatred are nothing more, in the middle of a meal, then the goad of desire larded with gentleness."

Because of drama in Picasso's work there is inverted drama in my own, e.g. a contrast of black and white becomes white and black. Grey on grey would remain bland. The contrasts I create highlight the dynamics in Picasso's work. Both together produce something even more extreme. Perhaps a true inversion would be to make a black and white drama into a grey blandness. But this would have produced a text of more limited interest.

I would suggest my artistic contribution is in the use of inversion. Future applications could be vast and numerous. There could be a transformation of swathes of literature into inverted versions. Jane Austen's "Pride and Prejudice" could become "Humility or Impartiality". Charles Dicken's "Hard Times" could become "Soft Spaces". And Leo Tolstoy's "War and Peace" would become "Peace or War". I must get writing …

REVULSION FREED FROM A HEAD LOCK

CHARACTERS

LH – LITTLE HAND

C – THE CHEESE

P – THE PIE/NUN/PRIEST

U – HIS UNCLE

M – SQUARE/MOUSE

L – THE LAPTOP

N – NOISE

TE – THIN EUPHORIA

FE – FAT EUPHORIA

VB – THE VENETIAN BLIND

ACT ONE

SCENE ONE

LITTLE HAND

Cheese amuse us. We are starving and want to hear our
Uncle's lies. Continue ramblings about faithful
relationships. Show the clean, smooth glove to the lady
passenger, despite her rudeness.

MOUSE

Now! Now!

LITTLE HAND

Yes, yes!

PIE/NUN

Drown me in your noise!

LITTLE HAND

Ha

MOUSE

Ha Ha

LAPTOP

Click Click

LITTLE HAND

Don't agree to squatting in a slum.
Let's be divided. Let's put Noise in a dress and take her
from the pudding in which she is slowly simmering.

THIN EUPHORIA

I'm not silent.

FAT EUPHORIA
>Nor am I.

CHEESE
>I dictate that my public preaching in my home, in open privacy, is for all to see, however far away, from whatever telescope.

LITTLE HAND
>That's a stupid, boring but delightful assertion. The Judge and jury are here, infernal fire. But you will cry helpless in the light from the squatters' rights.

NOISE (Putting on her dress)
>Oh Devil, I'm cold.

THE UNCLE
>I turned off the gas but it is still hot. How exciting!

CHEESE
>I'll open the window, its steaming up.

MOUSE
>Why not destroy that horrible old window, we want the cat and flies to come in.

PIE/NUN
>Give me the dirty polluting fresh air any day.

FAT EUPHORIA
>It's exciting.

THIN EUPHORIA
Louder – We rule the roost.

MOUSE
Hello, Hello, you are so ignorant of where we are.
The ABC

SCENE TWO

(Change of scene to bright dawn)

VENETIAN BLINDS (Flip up and down)
How calm. How delightful.
I can't say it is a good day for a fight … it's a Greek day,
a bountiful, cornucopia of a day in a Greek Vase – a day
of calm for my clear head (crying and sniffing.)

(Music of Louis Armstrong's "What a Wonderful
World" above the lights get brighter and flies land.)

ACT TWO

SCENE ONE

(Front of LUXURY'S Squat)

(the hands of the squatters are behind the lit windows slowly moving in pleasure)

HANDS OF WINDOW NO.3
Your pleasure, your pleasure your pleasure.

HANDS OF WINDOW NO.5
Your pleasure, your pleasure your pleasure.

HANDS OF WINDOW NO.1
Your pleasure, your pleasure your pleasure.

HANDS OF WINDOW NO.4
Your pleasure, your pleasure your pleasure.

HANDS OF WINDOW NO.2
Your pleasure, your pleasure your pleasure.

(the lights turn off and a donkey following a banana tied in front of its head passes the front of the squat as the light comes on.)

SCENE TWO

(Some scenery)

(A WOMAN brings a shower hose pipe and squirts the dirty windows to reveal from the neck up LITTLE HAND, THE CHEESE, THE PIE, HIS UNCLE, MOUSE, LAPTOP, NOISE, THIN EUPHORIA, FAT EUPHORIA, THE VENETIAN BLINDS.)

THE PIE / NUN
Dirty and grubby, staring blankly at a brick wall we are never prepared for the end of the Big Wheel of life.

LITTLE HAND
Pie/Nun, you are invisible!

CHEESE
Invisible to me too

LAPTOP
Invisible, invisible, saint / virgin.

LITTLE HAND (Ignoring the Pie / Nun)
Your ugly arm and twisted mouth, your crude bottom and deformed back, hilarious lips and ears a compost heap, shoulders a rock, and the wintery chest the stage of a London comedy club, your breasts a bowl of dog food, and your legs a mouldy baguette, and your _ and your compost heap of dead flowers the damp water of compost decomposition. And my poison, my buzzard, my wild animal, you revolt me, revolt, revolt, revolt.

THE CHEESE
Young virgin, great virtue.

LAPTOP
You know young boy you re in church.

HIS UNCLE
Carry on and I'll wash and stay.

PIE / NUN
Here is the dirt, the dirt, the dirt !

LITTLE HAND
A Saint !

CHEESE
Yes, a saint !

PIE / NUN
The dirt tastes disgusting, yuk, it tastes disgusting !

LAPTOP
Leave the dirt, put it down.

LITTLE HAND
Ugly old woman, I push you away.

LAPTOP
A Saint, huh !

(THE MEOW, purrs, and jumps from window to
window, shunning everyone, wet from the hose and the
squatter stay behind their windows naked in dirt.)

THE PIE / NUN alone is wearing a clean habit

PIE / NUN
We have no food, may God help us.

In comes the WOMAN WITH hammer nails and boards.
She begins to board up the windows.

ACT THREE

SCENE ONE

(White back blinds, curtains, white site blinds/curtains and carpet.)

LITTLE HAND

Instinct tells us that everything is worse than ice cream. I am indiscriminate, in a terrible, hot sticky night, a slap dash helping from the inconspicuous petrol station or ubiquitous super market.

The impersonality of shopping through a self-service till is awful and commonplace. The lifeless, humourless coldness of the shopping, empty of love, and, from start to finish, a revolting violence. The hot machine facing outwards and the cold slot burning the metal of the closed paradise adds all its impersonality to the festering skin.

The supermarket attendant's descent into ugliness, his subtle repugnance, freed from his uniform and the rock of his hatred, trap the black sludge of his stare away from the customer, its sweet smelling nakedness brought into the door of his personality, blunt from the rock of his shaven head. And if the electric guitar of his beautiful, rare silence and his weep, please the rough base of a landscape, it is nothing to do with modesty and his pleasing agreement to give his Desert of hate. The shield of a bunch of cabbages which he stacks on shelves is silent at his feet about the common cursing of the culprit. The saunter of the shoppers revulsion is felt, the sound that died one night in the stale cockerel of his clothes falls on the floor and jumps with full lungs on the wall. My clothes are different, they are dead. The vegetables at his feet have an aroma of perfume. I ignore the sound of his nostrils flaring, containing the stench of is punch, I drench off the flame of desire with the spit of his revulsion. The freezer is blameless.

*

SCENE TWO

(Scraping of the window)

SQUARE / LAPTOP
Nobody here !

LITTLE HAND
Go Away !

SQUARE / LAPTOP
It's rough here, Little Hand, Young girl, and the horrible stench of melted ice cream have a bad morning, I am here ! On the riverside I heard no noise but I left anyway to get my money to put into my current account.

LITTLE HAND
Apologise. Give me the money. My evening's misfortune. No food, not half this, nor half that. And the night's a white terror.

SQUARE / LAPTOP
It's hot !

LITTLE HAND
Get me a cup of tea. To chill my heart. House squatting fills me with joy because the slimy tenants, squatters disagree about paying and I love the neighbours, those fine people their thin dog sits away from my cat and they will upgrade the mouse, that I use for my computer. My toad is dead but my beer is good and summer will surely start with an abundance.

SQUARE / LAPTOP

The surest, slowest dead-end is to leave the cat facing the dog to leave the dog to play. Let them live, pull the hairs from them and let them wait and break clocks then freeze them and make meat ice-cream.

LITTLE HAND

She that cries first, cries worst. The dog alive and the person I hate cursing me, the squat will be dark as a pit and the famine will shrink and tighten the skins of the drums.

SQUARE / LAPTOP

Sanity of Sanities. Women are Sane. The Venetian Blinds that close the bottom of the black night that has long since fallen asleep I stay where I am and paste the floor with the green of the slime of the mould. Hateful night and this morning leave yourself hidden.

(She remains)

*

SCENE THREE

LITTLE HAND stands to the side an lauhts. Enter the
EUPHORIAS, THE UNCLE AND THE PIE / NUN

FAT EUPHORIA

(looking at LITTLE HAND)
She is as ugly as an asteroid. She is a nightmare stripping
paint from a canvas. Her skin is the simple tiles of a
supermarket and she has the air of a tin can kicked down
the street. Her soul is empty like a broken light bulb. Her
skirt is tight like a rotten cabbage. Her feet are opaque
fungus. The slugs of her lips free range the parking lot
that winces at her silent stare, and the vanilla ice-cream
texture that repels her absorbs a brutal darkness in her
backside that the sniff of a dog turns its nose away, like a
clam to the knife of an oyster hunter, which in my
repulsion knows the smell, sound and taste of him.

THIN EUPHORIA

I don't want anything to do with her.

PIE / NUN (laughing)

I hate her.

THE UNCLE

I was acquainted with a woman in London, a rubbish
collector/dustbin lady who was nearly blind and rejected
my advances. A horrible and poor woman. She insisted I
buy the breakfast, dinner and all meals. She made me
forget how to eat. She stayed close to me in a slum I
don't think standing up against a wall and being aware
aren't the same.

PIE / NUN (Pushing him away and laughing)
I hate her I hate her.

(PIE / NUN, UNCLE, THE TWO EUPHORIAS each put
paint brushes in their hands and begin to paint his head.
Until they have made his head white like a boiled egg
and it starts to drip. Through the blinds it is dark.)

PIE / NUN
No no no no no no no.

THE UNCLE
No no no no …

FAT EUPHORIA
N N N N N N N N N …

(goes on four times)

LITTLE HAND (staring wide awake)
The ice cream van over dead bones.

UNCLE
She is ugly ! No non o … where no … ah ! Where no no
isn't no no no no … hurrah

THIN EUPHORIA
Hoorah Hoorah.

PIE / NUN
No, No. I hate her. No no hate hurrah no no no hate her
no no hurrah hurrah.

(they have no paint on the and stand tall)

VENETIAN BLINDS, closing on this wonderful view
and quiver with delight in front of the table.)

*

ACT FOUR

SCENE ONE

(Clapping hands)

PIE / /NUN
I'm losing, I'm losing !

UNCLE
I'm not ! I'm not ! I'm not !

THIN EUPHORIA
I'm last ! I will be last !

LITTLE HAND
I'll lose my shirt !

SQUARE LAPTOP
I'll lost it !

CHEESE
I never win, I will lose.

NOISE
Forget it. Forget it !

FAT EUPHORIA
Even my Big Toe ignores me !

(The Queen card is dealt)

THE UNCLE
23. Bad luck. I lose !

SQUARE / LAPTOP
10 plus 14. That makes 24. I lose too.

THIN EUPHORIA
21. It's not my number. I lose the game.

PIE/NUN
Ace plus 10 plus ten. I lose the game. I'm never unlucky.

LITTLE HAND
7, 7, Hell's teeth. A complete loser at the bottom of the heap.

NOISE
5, 10, Helloo happiness blood, bones and butcher. I am the mistress of loss.

SQUARE LAPTOP
8, 4k Lose and I and my commiserations.

THE UNCLE
25. I am the loser. I am the loser, I am the loser.

CHEESE
26. I lose. So badly wrong.

THIN EUPHORIA
22 that's the cards, I lose !

FAT EUPHORIA
27, 27 I lose now, here.

VENETIAN BLINDS (slowly closing)

22, 23, 24, 25, 26, 27 We all lose ! We lose ! We lose !

(A clamour of pots over an empty fire. The rattle gets louder and louder and louder until it is a complete cacophony.)

ACT FIVE

SCENE ONE

LITTLE HAND (Stood pacing and texting on a mobile phone)

"Desire of the level calm of hate and calm of the sitting duck of sanity. Revealing of the crimson trapped by the sky flowers that reveal the suit softened with the poor bones killed by the desert breath of the man standing next to me. Spit the frozen fire of her heart whispering with pleasure all the sadness of freedom. Precise work of liquid sitting in the set jelly of his clear actions. The text that dictates the picture projected on the sun diary propping up, with its spine, the poppy flowers, protects the bird of love and the beak of ice of his desire will free in the colour of the rose sometime when the contented apple is not ripe with pain. The single sport of dancing washed with a different blue to his suit, the ice which clings to the agitation of his character mends the dissonance of the quiet silence of noise freed from paradise.

The opaque smile wiped from the wall closed to the calm stinks of soft bones on the hot nesting of hawks that give it. The white paint reveals the dry clouds that soothe the hammer with the colours of the painting, sold for dirt free regress, in the blunt revulsion to reject him from her legs, her lost weakness and her explicit feebleness to win him. I am sure to lose her living from my legs, rotten and sane."

Hateful text if you don't like. Deliberated over and left to simmer. Today or this morning or tomorrow, I will send it impersonally. Latte 1, latte 2, latte 3, one, two, three, and plus two plus three equals six lattes; one drunk, one sitting and the third poured down the drain. Feet stuck into bottom like a block lifted slowly to a field that stays sits temporarily on his gothic face of a fully formed gargoyle. Hands apart, the night raises the lightness of seconds into the sky, free of reflection. The skin worn gargoyles before the peace take his photograph, off the black softness of the absorbent granite of his pleasure. The silence of locked doors stroking their sober voices on smooth walls sticks to the day joyful sighs of pain. The nail fixings of dire and the sour aroma from his bed stop the flavour of his empty pot. Fixed feet, feet fixed to trouser legs and smoothed without concern on the hessian bed, placed gently on the bottom of the hammer striking the ground, create joyfully in a rough square foot the experiment to be tried. Sand softened with birds that spit the rock of the venetian blind that wakes on the promenade away from the salt of the sea washing from the doorway. The invalid desire, the transcendence of safety, the hope and the fears that keep him also stop him at the place of living despair like this agitation in a strange place on a "fear-red" bed.

PIE / NUN (Enters. Slowly walking)

Evening ! Evening. I bring celibacy I am dressed and full of food. Don't destroy my satisfaction with your hunger. I am full but am cold. I am a stranger and want no flea ridden vest. Do not kiss me or even look at me. It is not obvious but I hate you coming here in black gloves, like a guard in uniform to say good night and make you fear me and want to run from me, hateful enemy that I am and relative victim of my feelings for you, such a harsh hater of my offensiveness you are. Be bold, ignore me. And only once. Stop what you are doing. And now I will grow a wart on my finger to delight you.

(LITTLE HAND pushes her away with his foot)

PIE / NUN (stepping back towards him)
You are stupid at selfishness, I am dripping sweat. I will
get an ice cube !

(She stands centre stage and turns her back to the
audience and drinks cold water for 10 seconds.)

PIE / NUN
Aarg ! That's worse !
(She burps, messes her clothes and jumps into the air)

LITTLE HAND (gets out mobile phone)
More water? We have plenty of water. Water. Glasses
Cups. Ladels. Porridge. And here in my hand is my
predictable mobile phone and I will send you a text, that
you can digest, if you swallow it whole, gulp it down in a
moment in broad daylight when, all alone at the
afternoon. It is 20 words of irrelevance.
(He waves his phone.)

"The beautiful aroma contained in the organic fantasy of
the aesthetics, believed a posteriori, requires a promise of
purity and humility. With absent spouse and without
witness, I, a reckless and unrecognised writer, refuse
even a tiny part of my recklessness over everything when
free pleasure degenerates into unprincipled sensuality for
the infinite knowledge of the object on the chair, with
easing off the throttle, on the simple nature with free
thinking over the dreams of whimsy never viewed

before, just as hidden darkness of blindness over collapsing sloppiness."

"The vulnerable closet was empty of salt and nectar of ugliness and the worst of the rejects of the hoi polio standing, ignoring illusions of plucked down of adults stuffed cushions like ripe bird spewed laughter."

From the civilian watch the watches featured a partial fascination for the curves of the movement of the moon overhead. The banality of mice that made the smooth needle for pricking thumbs, kills the fully living sky so much that clouds fall from their landing and light dropped by legs fastens on the cemetery grounds and sticks to the tarmac of the road, where it binds together in a frustrating ignorance of the ordinary freedom the be free of the permanent expanse.

TART / NUN AND THE UNCLE (Entering)
Shu – We have nothing for you. Shu – go away - ... We have nothing !

LITTLE HAND
How awful; here we are sitting quietly and you entertain us with pure nothingness. Why don't you want us, Pie/Nun and you, Uncle, to hate your nothingness ?

UNCLE
What ! Dull nothingness ! Weeds ! You mumble that "Our pure nothingness ! We are nasty, we ignore you and you are polite to us. That is wonderful.

PIE / NUN
I never learn so will give you nothingness again.

LITTLE HAND
Yes, and always …

UNCLE
You, Pie/Nun I can never keep a secret from your father.
This is terrible. Dress in front of a scoundrel, a writer, a
hack … and dressed in your bare hands, it is lowbrow
and sweet, and it makes you a goddess and my muse, and
it gives you respectability of an old lady. Your father in
the morning at the pub will find this predictable,
respectable behaviour of a lady elevated to the highest
reaches of Little Hand's tradesman's workshop by her
purest thoughts.

PIE / NUN
Uncle, you are a blessing… and, also, do you have a
metal rod, or give me a stick. I will make a mess of
myself and then hide. I will stay. I am in a stranger place
and this man is an angel, virtuous, disciplined and an
Aryan.

(She goes to the lounge.)

LITTLE HAND
Now the Pie/Nun is staying, ignore me. She is sane and
wants us to think the worst of her with her self-
emollitions her self-harming like a servant. I hate her and
despise her. But that together with divorcing her, my
desert or monster, there is a quick and easy vision. Her
ugliness disappoints me and I am repulsed by her
fragrance, her slovenliness, her nakedness and her
naturalness delight my soul. Don't give my your opinion.
I am ignorant. Uncle do not speak to me.

UNCLE

I don't know her, your great enemy. I hated the sight of her when we were at school. She was always shown as a bad pupil in class. Her skin was unblemished and she worked hard to get it that way. Using creams and eating properly she was very careful. A clean person with combed hair, smelling sweetly and always alert. In her long, white gown, her light boots and her woven skirt, none of the men – young students, old men and ruffians, we couldn't see the ice and snow falling behind her as her gorgeous sound remained, the rough coal of the dried up well of age freezing the feet showing on the ground.

PIE / NUN

That adult smelled so bitter an foul.

UNCLE

I don't agree ! The Pie/Nun is a little old lady and an ugly woman !

LITTLE HAND

Her mind is a winter's day empty and dark and smelling of soil.

PIE / NUN

You hate her, Little Hand, Little Hand, it is not for you. You hate her, it is not good and your destiny is bland. Fear ! You are cursed. Bad luck but only in small quantities ! Are you staying, Uncle? We remain. So ! Little Hand, you are vindictive to me … the Nothingness, remember to take, generally, a small plate, rock , and vase of nothing.

UNCLE
Good day, Little Hand ! (they go out.)

LITTLE HAND
Two delightful fellows. (He stands and thinks)
"The hard yellow of the badge which reveals with its flat metal the violets of the uniform of a tamed weed in a garden bleeds rivers, the big horns from sky–blue hips folding their legs. Once the Men of Ribchester had to pay Seventy Pounds a Week !"

PIE / NUN (Comes from the lounge naked.)
Are they here ? Saying Nothing again. English stay. No one delights me. And you, I hate you as well. And we must be bad, my tiny little nothing. Now I am a whore, I will remain to hide my shrinking genitals away from nobody, and tar my hateful open space out of the day light village cowls.

LITTLE HAND (Standing and finding a kettle.)
I lost from my new jacket the rock salt pretzel with tucked in curves of the white darkness of the moon.

*

ACT SIX

SCENE ONE

(Scene takes place in the kitchen and lunge of the slum
of THE EUPHORIAS)

FAT EUPHORIA

The freeze made by my healthy rationality stops the
healing of the burn disdained by the opaque rock which
has left the yellow curve of the sun beam and condenses
it in funerary wreathes. I am everything and a fluid body,
free of the door of the freezer. I caress my landscape on
my buttocks and laugh the donation of my pleasure, at
doorways, open to judgment. My CHEMISE
OPPOSITE, fixed together by heaters loosened by my
breath, licks the mountain dew of my legs with the
ammonia of its caress pushing my suit from my hands
and my laughter from widow to window. The big bag of
nothing that I stole for Little Hand for nothing freezes
my feet. Growing flower in my stomach, hate is serious
at dice over the scales of his skin. The new ripping plant
which steadies the donkey and the lamb of the free Ferris
wheel of my revulsion joins up my meaty skin and
refuses it dead to the free hot feet of the long dead outer
space, breaking the frame of my door their lamb-like
fullness and the pond-like saturation. The tiny pit of trees
is restless for its past. We must not make a meal.

(Throws down newspaper).

A full half of German sausage, some butter, some
orange, some runner beans, pepper, wine, battered, deep-
fried 'til crispy, no devil ready for heaven, keep it hot;

type up a single version in Chinese digital and allow it to go runny for the octopus.

(Whispering up the chimney of the lounge)

Brother ! Brother ! Go away ! Go and don't help me make a mess and waft out the pure clean sheet. Take your time, brother, the deep fried ice cream is hot and freezes the top of the television set. This morning I stamped on the ice-cream a song which it will shout for all to hear, and don't' rudely rush the chains of the hedge a daisy for the flesh.

THIN EUPHORIA (All neat and clean sitting on a clean chair and holding a hair brush.)
    I stay close and am bored by the impatience I had in front of the wedding party, siting like a duck that the think bleacher and demolisher, who is profligate, wanted to remover from my head.

FAT EUPHORIA
    The moon.

THIN EUPHORIA
    Hate.

FAT EUPHORIA
    Oh, you are ugly !

THIN EUPHORIA
    When I arrived this evening from the flower bed of our flat, in time, in front of the door, I put on my light dance shoes from my legs and, jumping from the hot spring of

my delights, I was forced to swim in the mill pond. Facing my front, I curled up on the clean grass and instantaneously I closed my ears to free my laughter. My open mouth also issued the mitre of the brief sunshine of weeds.

FAT EUPHORIA
Breakfast is over.

THIN ANXIETY
Down with sorrow, hate and the winter !

FAT ANXIETY
Go away, make the pastry and don't touch the filling. The single flower of delight and of pleasure wants to say hello. And the seaweed waves quietly, living happiness over the warm mouth of fascination.

(She takes a spoon and gets a scoop of sauce.)

There is too much jam and sugar in this sauce. My uncle has a mouse which chattered its teeth in the morning.

THIN EUPHORIA
Please don't serve me any ice cream. The serious sweetness of these rough meals stops my refined need for sweet candies from breathing disinterestedly.

FAT EUPHORIA
I don't know that black fishnet stockings that I lost in the pub which I stole one wonderful night, my funeral, newly made and perfectly coloured, on the bottom of the couch, I lie flat in cold pleasure on top of the clean, quite

microwave oven. I don't know if my boss bought then last night to leave her husband.

THIN EUPHORIA
Close your eyes, the window is sauntering away. No one is trying to get out. Not even the flower girl. Or is it the Pie/Nun.

(Speaking to the PIE / NUN.)

Go away. Go away and starve. Be sad. We don't' want to hear the history of the Little hand. The Cheese left this evening, dark and delighted, covered in dry faeces and healthy, healed in the stomach with a tablet. He was laughing. We left him to his own happy state. He was whole and complete. He soaked up all the humidity and whispered beautiful poetry.

FAT EUPHORIA
Forget that the dog bit the cat in the morning.

THIN EUPHORIA
We threw the dog in the air in feathers, possibly duck feathers. It rained in the night. Very hot, and with a chill in the air.

PIE / NUN
Forget I'm full of hate. Her feet are smooth and soft and she donates money in the street. She is rich, and gave up work as an international jet pilot. It's wonderful and she needs nothing. She will welcome you and soothe you. Little Hand rejected me and now he is free. Close your eyes ! I need to hide in the cellar, I am pale and pasty.

Hate. Hate. Give me ten pounds, change it into Yuan and
keep it all. Welcome ! Never. Deepest sympathy for your
funeral, my enemies ! Horrible morning ! A slightly
awful night for us all ! Miserable old second and hello !
(She drops her robes, covers her face and crying falls
against the door.)

THIN EUPHORIA

An ugly boy, stupid, and normal. None of that goes
towards a good start.

FAT EUPHORIA

Be Quite !

(She puts a finger to her mouth and says "Shh !" All the
characters of the play slowly gather around)

And Cheese, go away. You are not allowed anything.
There is nothing here for you.

CHEESE

No thanks to you Sir !

THIN EUPHORIA

Little hand, away, don't question my answers, I keep the
standing table in the bedroom. I don't want any answers
to mathematics.

LITTLE HAND

Not enough and a little amount.

FAT EUPHORIA

Slightly bad !

THIN EUPHORIA
Slightly bad !

FAT EUPHORIA (Clearing the table and covering with a
table cloth)
Square Mouse, why did that stink ?

(SQUARE MOUSE cries)

FAT EUPHORIA
Slightly bad ! You know. There was the purse emplty of
paints. Not for you. Misfortune awaits.

THIN EUPHORIA
Pie/Nun, hide your stealings.

PIE / NUN
My bull's semen has dried up. No meat. No eggs. No
fish. And my bald skin has nothing to feed upon. My
yellow teeth, salty excrement and black caviar under my
feet, enlivened with athlete's foot. Fleshy fillings.
Diahorrea. Smooth hands and feet. The Queen's good.
And eyes unfurled with lemon and merengue. Naked
with indecency, dirty I strip awkwardly from the
laudable suits stolen from me. I am a virgin and faulty
prude and have two left feet on the dance floor.

FAT EUPHORIA
We take your pot of water and butterfly net. And then we
watch you flail on the dance-floor.

(Music plays and the PIE / NUN dances badly)

LITTLE HAND
> Don't open the new mattress in the foot-stool of devils and shake the sheets in the daffodils. Turn off the lights. Catch a crow with no effort guided by flowers and open freely the tents put up by trees.
>
> (ALL THE CHARACTERS start to dance by the door at the side room, it slowly opening, enters a black cube which sucks in the light of the room. The characters take out torches and crouch down by themselves. Shouting individually in cacophony.)

ALL
> Me ! Me ! Me!
>
> (On the black cube appear the letters of the word: "Everyone" ")

www.ingramcontent.com/pod-product-compliance
Lightning Source LLC
Chambersburg PA
CBHW061222180526
45170CB00003B/1118